Sales explained

All you need to know for sales success

Stephen Carroll

Copyright © 2021 Stephen Carroll
All rights reserved
ISBN 9798748699594

The characters and events portrayed in this book are fictitious. Any similarity to real persons, living or dead, is coincidental and not intended by the author.

No part of this book may be reproduced, or stored in a retrieval system, or transmitted in any form or by any means, electronic, mechanical, photocopying, recording, or otherwise, without written permission or the publisher.

Cover design by; Not just scribbles, Chester, UK

Printed in the United States of America

In writing this book I recall the many friends and colleagues along the way who have braved the countless obstacles on the road to sales success. I remember fondly each and every person. It would not have been possible to write this book without their experience, support, encouragement and vision.

Finally, a word of huge gratitude to my wife whose editing skills have been invaluable to say nothing of her patience and encouragement.

Contents

What is selling 1

Essential for success 3

Finding your customers 7

Preparing for the sale 13

Telephone sales 21

The sales call 35

Key steps of a sale 41

Elevator sales technique 49

Building relationships 55

Psychology of sales 72

Using psychology for sales 88

Understanding your customer 104

Structure you sales activity 109

Best practice for sales success 111

Customer services 123

Sales interview success 135

Concluding thoughts 146

What people are saying

'A very experienced and successful sales professional. In this book Stephen Carroll has compiled the essentials of sales in a practical and understandable manner.

No lofty or over theoretical sales strategies, just nose to nose, toe to toe selling. If you want greater success in sales I highly recommend this book.'

Koen Lim, Director, Marketing and Sales, Plasmacure, Netherlands

'An insightful read that delivers exactly what it promises - to impact the knowledge needed to become a more effective sales person.

Short chapters break down key concepts; offering them up in a way that's easy to digest and remember, plus use of hypophora and storytelling kept me engaged throughout.

A short investment in time that overdelivers.'

Rebecca Canty-Collins, Head of Local Marketing, Deliveroo

'For those starting out, new to the sales profession and to those who have been in the profession for as many years as I have, this book serves as a reminder of what makes a successful sales person. At a time where the world has seen significant changes and the way many work has changed forever, it reminds us of the core behaviours that some of us take for granted or may have lost with the pressures of time. An easy read, compelling and reassuring that people still buy from people they like and the need for quality relationships with our customers old and new should remain core to a successful sales person.'

Julie Clarke Head of Sales, Whitworths Ltd

'Stephen brings a wealth of experience in driving and delivering sales success – from ground to board level and everything in between. His knowledge and understanding are second to none and he has succeeded in encapsulating all of this wisdom in this little gem of a book. Whether you're a seasoned campaigner, driving sales at the corporate level, or launching your entrepreneurial dream from the kitchen table. 'Sales explained' is a 'must have'.

Whatever your situation – whether you're already fully immersed in sales, or aspire to success in this challenging and competitive sphere – do yourself a favour and get hold of a copy!'

David Cartwright MBE, MEd Chartered Fellow CIPD

Don't be afraid to start over again
This time you are not starting from scratch,
You are starting from experience

BIGGS BURKE

Preface

I have spent a large part of my life involved in sales.

I don't think it was something really intended; it just happened. I think this is probably true of most people whose careers have principally been in sales.

Generally people wouldn't set out in their career saying 'I want to be a sales person'. Yet everything has to be sold - everything in our house, our cars, the paint that decorates our life, the food we eat, the medications we take, even components - everything has to be sold.

This means that there has to be a huge army across the world responsible for ensuring that we have the right products and the right services in the right places.

Genuine sales is a noble profession and vital throughout our commercial world.

I was given an opportunity to work in an environment where I could learn about sales across a whole range of industries. In the eighties I was offered a job in sales and marketing recruitment.

In my formative years I learned the key skills required for sales in engineering, petrochemical, medical and scientific, construction, architectural, and business to business sales.

I have spent time in factories watching CNC machines turn out prototype parts, I have seen trucks being built, I spent time visiting companies manufacturing everything from air conditioning units to computers, and service industries from recruitment to contamination management learning about their businesses. I have listened to owners, directors and sales managers determine how best to sell their products, and this has enabled me to understand and create a structured approach to sales that I can now pass on to you. I will always be grateful to each of these business owners who taught me so much at that time.

My training was intense right from the start, often described as blue chip training working for a PLC organisation that required a very high standard of performance.

I will always remain indebted to the managers and directors who saw my potential and took me under their wing. Their mentoring was never an easy ride both for my sales development and subsequently my management training but they provided me with a comprehensive skill set that I could take with me and develop throughout my subsequent career.

In the nineties I founded my own Company. We decided that we could provide an enhanced service to clients looking to recruit sales people across the broad range of industries. That Company today is an International organisation and I am hugely proud of their success. During my career I have trained and mentored many sales professionals and managers who have gone on to greater success. For me this has become the greatest achievement of my career. I owe it with gratitude to those who gave me my earliest chance of success.

Sales Explained is my way of sharing what I have learned along the way so that you can be successful too.

So, join me and I'll explain all you need to know for sales success. As we progress on our journey we will explore the huge benefits that companies can derive from selling their products effectively and efficiently.

It will benefit your business, transactions and even your personal life!

Introduction

When we want to get something right we say that we need to go back to basics. In our ambition to be something special, to be successful, to build our business we can become consumed by this ambition and forget that every voyage of discovery starts with the first step. Going back to basics is like a father helping a toddler to walk. He picks the child up, stands them on their feet, they take a few tentative steps and fall onto their bottom. He picks them up again, they toddle forwards and fall again. He has infinite patience happy that the child is beginning to walk. So in sales or any business venture we need to remind ourselves that we are like toddlers learning as we go taking one step at a time using our experience from the last time to stay on our feet that bit longer.

I have purposely written this book in simple step by step, topic by topic form so that you can use it for easy reference. There are no big explanations, just the basics plain and simple. You can keep it beside you as a companion or it can be used for team work.

The important thing is we remember the basics and that we take sales one step at a time. This is true whether you are setting out on your sales career, running a business or even if you have amassed great skills in your field of expertise and you have been selling to customers for many years. All of us can benefit from going back to basics.

This is not the book to learn about using social media for sales or digital marketing. You can look elsewhere for experts in this field. I am focusing on the skills required for selling to customers either face to face or by telephone. Sales direct to the customer.

Selling is simply about looking after your customers. It's that easy.

Many entrepreneurs go out of business because they lose sight of the small things: putting their customers at the centre of their activities, managing costs, developing their staff.

This book is about going back to a few essentials that could considerably increase your success.

I hope you enjoy it.

Note to readers

My purpose in writing 'Sales explained' is to make selling accessible to everyone.

The best way to use this book is to read it through for the big picture and then keep it as a companion as you sell to your clients.

These pages will provide help and direction whether you are the director of a firm responsible for selling to your customers, or a small business owner where the responsibility for sales is shared between directors and technical managers. It can also provide a structured course for someone new to sales with the need for good basic training, a valuable guide for an administrator, secretary or customer services person engaged to a greater or lesser extent in selling to customers.

The principles and the structure needed for sales success are simple and work for everyone.

Many people are obliged to transfer their existing skills and experience to new markets caused by economic change. For example the need to move from retail sales to business to business sales (B2B) or business to consumer sales (B2C). All the new skills you require are available to you in the following pages and will give you the head start you need.

Many new channels and outlets have emerged for the promotion of our products and services. Even with the rapid growth of online marketing and social media the basics of selling remain unchanged.

In these times of increasing competition, where only the most capable companies survive, your success will depend on providing the best possible solutions through competent selling.

Establishing trust with your client is better than any sales technique

What is selling?

The dictionary says this:

'Sales is the exchange of a commodity for money'

So, it is a transaction where the sales person provides something that the purchaser needs and the latter, in turn, pays an agreed sum for the product or service. When you think about this you begin to realise that everything is either sold or bought. Your food in the supermarket, the ingredients that make up the food items, the car you take them home in, all the components that go to make up the vehicle, each brick of your house and so the list goes on.

It's fair to say that Sales makes the world go around! We all use sales techniques in our lives as a matter of course.

For example: You call the plumber because you need a pipe fixing. He says he can come next week but you need him tomorrow, so you ask:

'What are the chances of you coming tomorrow?' 'Well, OK then, I'll come tomorrow' 'How much will it cost?' 'I can get the job done for you for £50 plus VAT' 'Great! See you tomorrow!'

This is a typical example of a sale, a transaction.

You need his services;

He accommodates your needs;

A price is agreed.

It is much the same in commerce.

The secret to sales success in the commercial world is both structure and approach.

In each chapter I will explain clearly all you need to know for your sales success. If you follow the principles carefully we will together reach our objective of equipping you with a structured approach to sales which will guarantee success.

Essentials for sales

Why should a client buy from me?

Success in sales is not a matter of chance. Yet most people who embark upon the daunting task of being responsible for sales worry about being successful or rather about the prospect of not being successful. In my earliest days of sales I was frightened to pick up the 'phone to speak to a real life client. Fear of failure haunted me. In those days, in the eighties, selling professionally had yet to evolve.

Throughout my career I have seen the reputation of selling develop from being a hard nosed, quick deal role to the relationship building and solution finding profession it is today. A revolution and an evolution that needed to happen. You will only be successful in sales when opportunity and preparation come together.

Before you even go out to find a customer you need to be sure, in your own mind, about the products and services that you intend to offer and who could benefit from them. The best way of thinking this through is to ask yourself this question:

What is my UNIQUE SELLING POINT?

Otherwise known as your USP.

What are you offering that your competitor isn't able to offer? It might be your competitive price, the quality you can offer, the quantity you can provide, The additional services and support you can offer, the availability or your products and services. You need to up-sell this point so that you can steal a march on your nearest competitors.

Building blocks of the sale

So that we can add structure to the way we sell we are going to take a look at the key building blocks of a sale. I'll list these with a short explanation here but later we will look at them in greater detail as we progress.

Here they are:

Planning the sale

What are the components of the sale that I need to prepare? How will I find the decision maker and make contact?

Structuring the sale

There is a high correlation between structured sales and results. The preparation and planning of the sale will directly affect the outcome. 70% of high performing companies focus on a structured skills set for their sales staff.

High performing companies are more likely to guide their sales activity through a structured sales process.

Managing the sale

The first impressions you give are key to whether you have a real chance of gaining the sale or not. These are confirmed in the first few seconds of meeting a potential decision maker. People buy from people they like; people buy from people they trust. If you are organised and have prepared well for the sale then you will be in control and conduct the negotiation efficiently.

Converting the sale

Provided that you are well able to provide solutions to the decision maker and adequately address their concerns then you will put yourself in a good position to achieve the sale. The closing of the sale will depend on the way in which you have conducted the sale and the achievement of the business will depend on your skills to manage an efficient close.

These factors will be explored as we progress through the course.

Finding your customers

The starting point for almost every sales person is to ask the question: 'Where am I going to find my customers?'. We are all familiar with the empty desk, a telephone, a sheet of paper or perhaps a computer - what next? Perhaps the 'phone will ring and a new client will ask for my products?

No, it doesn't work like that! Sales is down to your diligence, perseverance, tenacity and hard work. There's no way around it. However, I'm going to give you a plan to find your customers.

The overriding objective of every business is the desire to turn over a healthy profit, that's how businesses grow and flourish. But how exactly is this achieved? Sales is the answer. The ultimate goal of every business, whether large or small, international, national or local, is to make sales and make a profit.

Where are your customers?

Here's a thought that we should all keep in mind when we want to find customers:

It's not who you know that counts; It's who knows YOU and what they think of you.

Every business and product requires a different approach, that's why a variety of techniques need to be tried, so you can find what works for you, your business and your sales growth.

Two questions we have to ask are:

How do we find our customers currently?

How would we like to find our customers in the future?

Word of mouth

Clearly one of the best ways of finding new customers is by word of mouth.

There is nothing better than a recommendation. It's safe, usually dependable and comes with the next best thing to a guarantee.

However, it's important to encourage recommendations. If you have done a good job for someone always ask if they know anyone else who might need the same kind of service.

Always follow up the recommendations you receive.

Good reputations are hard earned but can be lost very easily.

Networking

These days networking has become almost the norm for achieving new customers.

Now that 'cold calling' has become somewhat disagreeable to many and possibly unlawful, new and more fruitful ways of generating new customers have been developed.

Networking is closely related to 'Word of mouth' recommendations.

There are many networks available around the country for business leaders nowadays.

It is important to choose the most suitable based on the kind of companies that attend particular network groups because they are all different and attract a variety of business types.

Again, consistency and relationship building is key.

It is only as you become known and gain a reputation as someone people can depend on that you will start to gain referrals and potential opportunities.

Enquiries

These are clearly the easiest way to find new customers but sales professionals need to be careful not to squander an opportunity. Every enquiry should be taken very seriously and followed up on right away to demonstrate to the potential customer that you care about them and are efficient in providing a solution.

I should add that, in order to gain further enquiries, you need to have a presence. Potential customers need to know who you are, what you do and be able to verify that you do a good job. The latter is more of a marketing question but remember that reputation in the market place is a vital function of selling and it needs to be safeguarded carefully by the way you look after your existing customers.

Online enquiries

More and more of our business is being achieved online mainly through having a web sales portal. In this current way of business achievement we still have to use the tried and tested methods of generating quality leads and providing a valuable sales process for customers.

A word about Google Ad words

Many Companies have found that they have lost a lot of money using Google Ad words. This is because they have tried using this marketing method without understanding it correctly. Putting both resources and effort into using Google Ad words can generate significant leads.

Google Ad words reward good advertisers as they become more efficient.

Then, of course, the same principles of sales apply being careful to attend to each and every enquiry quickly and efficiently using a structured sales approach.

Your website is a tool that again requires resources and effort if it is to be used efficiently. Many companies produce a nice website because everyone 'has one' and then they leave it there, online, hoping that it will produce something. That's unlikely! How will anyone see it unless you drive traffic to your website? Website optimisation is important if you want to generate sales leads through your site but beware as there are a lot of spurious businesses out there who claim to offer website optimisation but don't efficiently drive enquiries to your business.

Advertising

There are the usual ways of placing advertisements for your business. The argument you often hear against placing adverts is that you can't guarantee a response for the money you invest. This is true but also true of much of the budget we allow for finding new customers.

That is why I want to help you make the most of every business opportunity that comes your way and to help you maximise profits from sales.

Preparing for the sale

We've already thought a little about how we approach selling in terms of our attitude of mind. We are now ready to put in place the building blocks for effective selling that will have an incredible effect on building your confidence to deal with customers and to become effective in sales.

Asking open questions

One of the most important learning points for someone in a sales role or any business role is to ask open questions.

What is an open question?

An open question is a question that elicits a response that provides information.

This contrasts with a closed question which leaves you without any more information.

Generally, these questions will begin with 'Who, What, When, Where, Why, How'.

For example:

What's the weather like today?

How often do you go into town?

Neither of these questions can be answered with *'Yes'* or *'No'*

In answer to the first: You have to provide information on the current weather situation.

'Well, it looks like rain; it's a lovely sunny day.'

Or in the second question: How often do you go into town?

'Not very often, just when I need to go to certain shops'.

You have information that provides answers to your questions.

However, if I were to ask these as closed questions:

Is it raining? No.

Are you going into town today? No.

Both of these questions can be answered with a simple 'Yes or No'.

I have no further information; I have not succeeded in gaining more knowledge and risk the conversation being terminated.

Have you ever listened to TV presenters and news reporters asking questions?

I'm often surprised by them. Their objective is to elicit information from their interviewee.

And yet, more often than not they make statements themselves first. They then realise that they have to ask a question, so they have to rephrase.

Eventually they get around to creating a question which is rarely an 'OPEN' question, so they fail to get a good response from their interviewee.

In sales, information is key, information is power, information enables you to create the conditions for a potential sale.

If you have information from your potential customer about their needs, their concerns and their objectives - then you can provide a solution.

***

The essential elements for success in a sale

We have been thinking about the elements of preparation necessary before the sale. We have described them as the building blocks to put in place for a successful sale.

But what about 'me' and my role in the sale?

The next task is to consider how I will prepare myself for the sale.

That is to say: what personal characteristics will I need to bring to the sale for success?

How did I *feel* when I was making contact with a potential client especially for the first time? Not having been in a commercial role until I took on my first sales job I found the whole experience of speaking with a 'real life decision maker' absolutely daunting. I was speaking with a highly experienced business person, yet I was in my first weeks in any kind of commercial role. I couldn't let the side down!

Whilst I had been trained on how to handle the sales call, how to phrase my introductions, how to ask questions, nothing prepared me for the actual conversation I found myself engaging in. This was for real, in real time and I was scared.

So how did I pull myself through in those early days?

The first indicator was that I knew that I had a pleasant character and I could use this to engage my interlocutor. I had enough confidence in myself and my experience dealing with people in ordinary life to know that I could 'warm' people up and get them talking to me. I found that most people were quite normal really. Whilst they didn't want to waste time on my call or my visit I had enough presence for them to listen and engage with me. There were always the difficult people who, no matter what you had to offer, took pleasure in giving you a hard time but in the main people were generally quite civil. In addition, they didn't want to miss out on something worthwhile so if I believed in what I was saying they would generally hear me out.

The second indicator I discovered was that I realised that I could influence most people I spoke with. There was something about the way I dealt with people, how I engaged with them, that enabled me to take them with me. All I really needed to do now was to hone my selling skills to be successful.

Key elements to prepare

What questions do I need to ask?
Presenting myself and my product
Likely objections I will encounter
My professionalism
Smiling and visualisation
Pace of call Intonation and volume

Clarity

'Sales is a transfer of feeling'

If you believe in your products or services then your listener will believe too.

Key influencers for your sale

Here are a few key influencers to help you prepare to make a sales call whether in person or on the telephone. Be comfortable, be enthusiastic, listen, be patient, believe, use humour, be confident.

So, let's take these one by one:

Be comfortable

Be relaxed when making a call, not always easy at first. Treat the call like you are calling a friend. Perhaps you should stand? Sometimes it helps. It is hugely important to get the opening of the call right.

Think about the opening of your call. Be clear, state the reason for your call. Use a formal greeting until invited to be less formal or they use your first name.

Example:

'Mr Jones? Good morning. My name is …

The reason for my call today is…

Don't ask 'How are you?' as callers tend to these days. You don't know them and it's irrelevant to ask.

Be enthusiastic

Be keen to get into a discussion with your client. If you are keen to find a solution, he will be too.

Listen patiently

Be prepared to listen. Do not rush the call. You may find an angle of interest to the client that you can help with. Control the call, allowing enough time to cover all the points you need to have an open and shared conversation.

Believe

Show that you believe passionately in your products or services. Belief is vital to selling. You need to convey this through your voice and expression. Narrate a story to convey your understanding, your belief and willingness to help.

Be confident

Along with belief has to come confidence. If you know you can help, tell your prospect. If you aren't sure, tell them how you think you might be able to help and present a plan.

Be proactive - think of solutions. Your confidence will set the tone and carry the call.

Use humour

Don't take yourself too seriously! Have a little fun and help your prospect to relax. Self deprecating humour works well.
Don't tell jokes!
Make sure you break the ice especially with more formal customers.

Exercises for you to try:

Write down your pitch to a new customer to introduce your products or services.
Think through how you will find the real decision maker and get through to them. Open your call and present the reason for your call.

Telephone sales

This is a vital skill to be acquired by anyone in business.

Even in these days of technology and online communication we still need to talk to our customers. Going back to basics is key to sales success and the humble telephone remains a vital tool for anyone in sales.

I sat behind my new desk way back in the mid-eighties. There was the large expanse of desk in front of me and on the left hand side a white telephone. Fortunately, technology had progressed sufficiently to push button dialling which meant that I would be saved from the prospect of one finger dials that had gone before. I sat there thinking about the calls I was required to make and it filled me with dread. From the list of potential clients I picked my first call. I chose one with a nice sounding name or something I could identify with to make the call easier for me. I picked up the 'phone and dialled. I made a mistake in my dialling which provided a moment of relief as I re-dialled. As I waited for the call to be answered I could sense the handset shaking against my ear and my heart was pounding. The call was answered with the Company name and I launched into my request for the name of the decision maker.

Telephone skills are becoming even more necessary despite a permanent move towards online selling where organisations are required to sell directly to the consumer. The majority of businesses have not yet fully appreciated the need to focus on the recruitment and sales training of their staff to compete efficiently in the business to consumer (B2C) market.

Many sales professionals have difficulty selling via the phone.
Selling to customers on the telephone is still an essential way to do business these days. We carry mobile phones all day so the phone is hugely important for getting business.

Some questions to consider:

Do you ever initiate sales over the phone?
How often do you speak to your clients over the phone?
How do you feel about using the phone to sell?

Preparing to make a telephone sales call

Whilst achieving the sale is our key objective we put a plan in place to ensure that we take all the necessary steps towards achieving our goal.

We should not be hasty or see the sale as our own primary objective but a benefit for our customer. In the past sales people gained an unfortunate reputation for being 'pushy' and' hard nosed' in certain industries. We think of the glazing industry or photocopiers in particular.

This reputation arose for two reasons:

They cared less about their customers than achieving the sale
They refused to put time and effort into providing a solution that would lead to a sale

Whether you are making your sale on the telephone or face to face the basic skills remain the same. However there are important factors that you must consider if you are to make sales successfully over the 'phone.

Make it personal

When we sell to customers over the telephone we must ensure that we project our personality. This may appear more tricky if our client doesn't have the benefit of meeting us personally. Nonetheless, we have to ensure that we take the necessary steps for our client to get to know us and we have to build their trust in us.

The mechanics

There is a clear disadvantage to selling over the telephone in that we cannot use body language as part of the sale like we can if we are face to face with our client. However, there are ways of mitigating this using some very basic techniques which we will take a look at now.

Visualise the decision maker

We all create a picture in our mind's eye of the person we are talking to. This is a good thing!
This helps you deal with a real person and will encourage you to make the call more relaxed.

Be professional

Do you dress as a professional business person, even when making sales calls?
Build your own esteem by being professional.
Sit up at your desk or even stand to make a call.
Be well prepared and don't waste words (we will look at preparation for the call later).
Your recipient will pick up on your professionalism, your enthusiasm, your approach.

Smile and be happy

When you are making a call.
This will add to your enthusiasm and make you cheerful.
Sales is a transference of feeling and it will transfer to your caller on the other end.
If you are enthusiastic and cheerful your listener will gradually respond even if they have come to take your call reluctantly or have other pressing thoughts in their mind.

Pace of the call

Control the pace of the call.
Don't rush or speak too quickly. You will loose your gravitas or, worse, the importance of your call.
On the other hand, don't be too slow or boring in the conversation! Listen carefully and mirror the person on the other end.

Intonation and expression

Consider your intonation and your expression to convey your enthusiasm but keep it controlled.
'That's really great!'
'OK, so to conclude…'
Vary your intonation, your expression and the volume you use to highlight the points you need to emphasise, to regenerate interest in a point or to bring your call to a conclusion.

Never apologise

Never apologise during a call except at the beginning if you are told you have interrupted something.
Do not apologise for your product or service, for information you want to impart or for interrupting.
Instead make the other person feel that you are helping or doing them a favour.
Apologising loses your control over the business call.

Always clarify

Be clear and concise. Make sure you summarise your key points. Check your listener's understanding of the key points you make.

Preparation of the sales call

You must have noticed by now how much emphasis I put upon preparation?
Even from my earliest days in sales I wouldn't let myself begin a call without adequate preparation. You only get one bite at the cherry and if you flunk the initial moment of introduction you are most unlikely to recover the conversation.

One of the most likely causes of failure to achieve a sale is a lack of preparation.

Poor preparation means a poor first impression - not knowing who you need to speak with; how to ask for the right person; inability to state clearly the reason for your call.

Up to now we have explored the need to prepare for a sale by the way we ask questions and the key factors that are required for a sale to be successful.
We have also looked at some of the mechanics of conducting a sale over the 'phone.

Now, we are going to pay attention to the preparation necessary for our sales call.

My desk

They say that an uncluttered space makes for an uncluttered mind.
The initial step you need to take before starting your preparation for a sales call is to tidy your desk. It might sound a little basic but I would strongly make the point that it will often mean the difference between sales success and failure.

If you get rid of all the things that do not relate to this particular call or this particular client then you can focus on your preparation clearly. Aim to have your key points about the client, their needs as you understand them and how you can best provide a solution so that you can better organise your sales call. Anything more is clutter.

If you have information relevant to the call and you can't find it during your conversation with the client due to a lack of organisation you will appear disorganised and incompetent. You can't expect to build the confidence of your prospect saying 'it's here somewhere!'

A tidy desk is a tidy mind. Always work on that basis and it will be a vital tool in your box.

***

Good prospect : Bad prospect

When we are relatively new to sales we have a raw enthusiasm for what we might achieve. I have experienced this myself and I have seen it time and again in young sales people when I have been training them.

Prospecting for new business can be tough. It requires great discipline and tenacity to keep going. As someone once said to me:
'Every call you make you are one call closer to your next deal'.
When you have been calling all morning with nothing to show for it in terms of tangible results and then a potential prospect says that they are interested in your products or services, the natural reaction is to jump in and try to obtain the business opportunity to hand.

But is this good business?

Just because this prospect shows interest it does not mean that a sale is at hand. It might be, but our potential sale still has some way to go at this point.

The kind of sales conversations I had been involved in myself earlier in my career and have observed many times in others can potentially waste a great deal of time.

Sales professionals need to ask enough pertinent questions to qualify their prospect.
Typically a dubious prospect will show interest in your product and ask interested questions. This energises the sales person to build the relationship. In many situations like this the prospect will try to offer a derisory amount for the product. Another may indicate that there may be some interest at some later date, say next year.

This is not a good business prospect.

There is nothing to suggest at this point that the sales person should pursue this prospect.
It may be better for them to file the interest shown and move on to the next call.
The sales person needs to ask the right questions to 'polarise' the call.

For example:

'What is your timescale for going ahead with this purchase?'
'What budget do you have available for your project?'
'Who else is involved in the decision?'

The sales person needs quality information to be able to decide whether to continue with the prospect or not.

What do I need to know?

Here are the key open questions we need to answer:

WHO is the decision maker?
WHAT is their role in the Company?

HOW will my products / services assist them?
WHAT are my objectives in the call?
HOW will I begin the call?

What questions do I need to ask?

Do I have the questions I need to ask ready, and to hand, to achieve my objectives from the call?
Remember to always ask OPEN QUESTIONS to illicit information.

Some examples might be:

'Good morning! Who is the person I would need to speak with concerning 'Widgets'?...
Is he in the office today?
What time will he be free?

Or you have already identified the decision maker and you call them:

'Mr Jones? Ahh, good morning. I would like to have a quick word with you about your 'Widgets';
*'**Where** do you source your raw materials currently?'*

Presentation stating the reason for your call is important because it clarifies the reason for your call and you aren't trying to hide anything, something decision makers will appreciate.

You can acknowledge that the decision maker's time is precious and that your call won't take long but be ready with an important open question that you need the answer to such as:

'What would your thoughts be on trying another supplier if we could provide a quality product and save on costs?'

It would be most likely that the decision maker will be listening to you by now.
All this is part of your sales presentation:

You are professional
You aren't wasting the decision maker's time
You have something worth considering

Now that you have the ear of the decision maker you will need to capitalise on your opportunity. Don't waste it by a poor presentation of your product or services.

Rehearse the presentation of your products and services so that you will be clear, concise, enthusiastic and engaging to the decision maker. Remember, you only get one chance!

Likely objections

It would be odd if the decision maker simply said 'Yes, that's fine!' Without asking any questions or raising any concerns. So expect points to be raised.

When a decision maker raises a concern you should take it as a buying signal. People who aren't interested don't put themselves out to ask questions or raise concerns, they just tend to move on.

Have I thought through their likely objections and do I have suitable responses to handle these?

Be well prepared and have suitable solutions to any possible concerns a potential customer might raise.

Conclusion and close of the sale

This is totally achievable over the 'phone.
The key elements remain the same as if you were speaking face to face.

When you have presented your products and services, you have listened carefully to the decision maker's response and you have handled any concerns the decision maker may have satisfactorily, then you can continue towards the close of the sale. Ensure that your decision maker is happy with all that you are offering and there are no remaining concerns.

You can then move to the close of the sale.

We will look more closely at closing the sale later in the book.

Exercises to try:

Prepare a presentation for your own product / service to a new prospect. Present to a colleague

Make notes together and see how you can improve your sales presentation

Try to anticipate likely objections you might face from a customer Find ways to handle these objections

Try closing the sale in different ways

The sales call

'Phone or in person

The same principles apply to structuring a sales call whether it is conducted over the phone or face to face.

There have been occasions in the past when I have scheduled sales calls or had them organised for me. Sometimes the calls can be arranged for the sales person and without due care. They can put time pressures on the sales person, perhaps not leaving enough time to find the clients' offices and be ready for the appointment. I recall in my own experience being stuck in traffic with the bare minimum of time available to find the premises of the Company I am due to call upon. There's nothing worse than being late or even arriving at the last minute. In those circumstances you have little or no time to compose yourself and prepare your first impression. This can directly influence the sales person's chance of success. Whether you are making your own calls or someone is making them for you ensure that enough time is provided so that there is no rush and nothing is left to chance.

Selling face to face is the same as selling on the telephone. We use the same basic structure to achieve our sale whether on the 'phone or in person. However there are additional points to consider when attending an appointment with a client.

So, what differences are there selling to someone who is present with you?
Let's take a look…

Preparing to make a sales call in person

The image you convey from the moment you arrive at the potential customer's premises has a direct affect on the outcome. Don't forget that they are expecting you! It is quite possible that they will observe you leaving your car and entering the building. So don't faff around with paper or drop your things as you leave your car. Arrive with all your paperwork and props pre-planned and well organised.
It is well known that decision makers call upon other team members for their opinion about you as you pass through their offices. This means that you should regard everyone in the organisation as influential to your sale and build the right kind of relationship with each of them.

Receptionists are important gate-keepers so you should give them due regard and earn their approval on the way in.

Remember that these people are also valuable sources of information which can have a direct bearing on the outcome of your sale.

You may well be making future 'phone calls to the Company and this person may be the person you regularly need to speak with. Build the right kind of relationship and they will help you with vital information such as the whereabouts of the decision maker.

Dress for the occasion

If you are visiting a factory or a builder's yard perhaps a suit and tie isn't necessarily required but don't assume that 'dressing down' is the right approach either.

Research the culture of the prospective company ahead of your visit. If you can't be sure then appear more formally. It's always better to show respect in the way you present yourself.

First impressions count

Perhaps you have previously spoken with the decision maker on the 'phone or with the receptionist who was your first contact.

What kind of impression have you already left?

This is important!
Remember what we talked about when making a sales call?
Have you built a good rapport?
This will help you now.

So, you are walking into your prospect's building for the first time. How are you going to handle this?

First, be confident and professional. Not over assertive - just professional. Be decisive.
Walk up to the receptionist and announce yourself and state the reason for your visit.
Be warm, smile and engaging, but remain professional.

'Hello, my name is John Smith and my Company is 'UK Widgets'
I have an appointment at 10am with Mr Steve Brown.'

When you meet the decision maker be warm, friendly, inviting and professional. A strong handshake creates a good impression.
Engage in a little small talk on the way to the office perhaps about the weather, traffic and so on. Perhaps complement them on their offices.

When you arrive in the decision makers office wait to be asked to sit down.
Caution:

Don't invade their space by putting your things on the desk
Don't take over the conversation launching into a sales pitch

Professional enthusiasm

They key to developing a good rapport with a client is how well you build the relationship. It doesn't matter how you feel, whether you are tired, demotivated, frustrated by some event earlier in the day. When you meet your customer you need to be enthusiastic.

I have an expression I like to use: *professional enthusiasm*.

By this I mean, when you meet your customer you put aside any negative thoughts or feelings.
As you approach your customer's office or even when you pick up the 'phone to call a client you smile and turn your whole demeanour into someone who is naturally enthusiastic and enjoys every encounter with a customer.
Anything less is unprofessional and will jeopardise your sales opportunity.

Points to remember:

Be professionally enthusiastic
Listen carefully to the decision maker for clues to their views
Look out for little buying signals that they may disclose
Wait to be invited to make your presentation
Thank them for the opportunity

Key steps of a sale

Now we arrive at the heart of selling

Effective selling is about being in control. The effective sales person is all the time in control of the sale. If your preparation is sufficient, a quality relationship with the client has been established and the options to provide a solution to the client have been carefully considered, then the sale can progress. Not every decision maker will be compliant in accepting your plan for a sale and so a subtle approach will be essential. Many of them will have worked hard to achieve the position they hold in the company or have built a business from scratch with sheer hard work. The sales person needs to respect this in dealing with the decision maker. However you must meet them on a level playing field to earn their respect in return. We need to adapt to the character of the decision maker. Individuals can be very different. I have found myself on occasion speaking with the managing director of a multi-national organisation and later with the manager of an East End of London plant hire company. I had to learn to be both engaging and credible with both. This isn't always easy and it will test your ability to adapt.

Both types of decision maker will have a certain pride in their work and business. Generally they will want to talk about their operation. Both will want to test that you are worth their time.

It is not a waste of time to listen to these decision makers. As you encourage them to open up you will gain vital nuggets of information that will help your sale. Always make notes during a conversation, listen carefully and react with interest to their comments and at the same time plan how you will achieve the sale.

It is time to take a look at the key steps in a structured way.

I make no apology for taking you right back to basics at this point because we all need to return there each time we conduct a sale.

Remember that sales is at the heart of every commercial transaction.

Sales makes the world go around and sales are conducted millions of times a day from buying a loaf of bread to financial transactions worth millions.
It's all sales!

The key steps of any sale remain the same.

So, let's look at them in more detail so that you can have a clear structure to your sale.

The structured KEY STEPS of the sale

Identify the decision maker
Present your product
Create urgency
Handle any objections
Close the sale

Let's look at these in more detail.

Identify the decision maker

Your research and planning for the meeting should have helped to identify the decision maker but be prepared when you start the meeting.

Who is the decision maker here?
Are you facing a group of people, two perhaps, or more?
Identify which one is the decision maker and focus your attention and tactics towards that individual.

Present your products or services

Present your product with care and enthusiasm. Clearly state:

The **FEATURES** unique or distinctive features of your products or services
The **ADVANTAGES** your products or services have for your clients
The **BENEFITS** of your products and services providing quality, ease, efficiency, satisfaction
What does your product have that your competitor's products do not have?
What is you USP? Your unique selling point?
For example - price, quality, quantity, availability.
Be concise, be tactful.

Create a sense of urgency

Everything sells at some point, but if you are able to give your potential buyer the impression that they really must take the item now before someone else does, so much the better.

Creating a sense of urgency tactfully really does help, and you can do this in a non-pushy way by saying things such as:

'These products are in high demand at the moment, I can't guarantee they will be here in a few days'

Alternatively:
'We've had a lot of interest in this, I'm sure it'll sell very quickly'.

Use narrative to assist you

Tell your potential buyer about how thrilled a previous customer was with this product and how you've built a great relationship.
By showing examples of how a product or service has improved a customer's results, you are more likely to close the sale.

Handle any objections

Less experienced sales people worry about an objection. An objection is clearly a buying signal. If they weren't interested they wouldn't pursue a concern. It's a positive thing!

Objections might simply be a lack of information:

A fair concern such as price or a perception issue
It could be a hidden objection such as a preferred supplier
It could be a lack of knowledge about their priorities this year

If a customer is giving you the opportunity to address a concern - be grateful!
It's good news! Tell them that you are happy to address their concern.
Empathise with the customer's viewpoint and concerns.

Qualify and isolate objections

Qualify your client's needs. Be sure you have understood correctly.
Ask, probe and confirm to ensure that you have got to the bottom of his concerns and that they have been addressed.

Isolate the key objection: *'So then, are you saying that the only reason you are unsure about going ahead is.. price / delivery etc.*

Reconfirm the value and benefits to them

Back it up with customer references, again use narrative. Then you can overcome their concern and move to close the sale.

Close the sale

Once the customer is engaged with your product and the sale, moving to the close should be relatively straight forward.

So, what are our options for closing the sale?

There are around 4 or 5 real options available to us:

1. *Direct close*
   'So, what are your thoughts on going ahead with the order?' This enables the decision maker to decide on their terms not yours.

2. *Assumptive close*

   'All we need to do now is to complete the order form and we'll get everything organised.' This is an easy way for the decision maker to go ahead without having to confront a decision.

3. *Alternative close*

   'So are you you going to go for product A or product B?' It's a choice of either/or. This makes it easier for the decision maker to decide one or the other.

4. *Reverse close*

   'So, is there anything that would stop you from signing the order today?' If 'no' you've got a deal.

5. *Deferred close*

   If you have to! Something like: 'So, you've said you like what you see today and there's no reason not to go ahead. We'll discuss the details or purchase, implementation and dates.'
   The deal is there for a later date.

Elevator sales technique

This is not new but a well tried technique to help the sales person focus clearly on communicating their aims and objectives in a sale. I think it's worth reminding ourselves of its value as we discuss 'communicating our message'.
As sales people we have all experienced being put in the position by a prospective client who is clearly focused on his own schedule which you have interrupted and they say something like:

'I've just two minutes. Make it quick!'

This can cause us to panic. So we need a technique in our capability to prevent us from panic. You have a tiny opportunity to get your 'foot in the door' for a later chance of business.
Try this method to see how good you are at communicating with your potential buyer when you don't have the luxury of time to make your sale.

The technique

First, with some preparation in advance as always:

IDENTIFY your target decision maker
EXPLAIN what you do
COMMUNICATE your USP your unique selling point
ENGAGE with a question
CLOSE with a plan of action

Let us imagine an unexpected sales opportunity arises. You've bumped into a former client at the airport.
After exchanging pleasantries, they ask who you are now working for.
You open your mouth to speak - you pause - where do you start?

The Elevator pitch is so called because your pitch needs to be succinct enough to last no longer than a ride in an elevator - about 20 to 30 seconds.

The key points

Your pitch must be a brief, persuasive speech that you can use to spark interest in what your organisation does.

You can also use it to create interest in a project, an idea or a product.
It needs to be succinct, while conveying important information.

Crafting your elevator pitch

So, to craft a great elevator pitch you'll need to follow these steps:

IDENTIFY your goal - what outcome do you need?
EXPLAIN   what you do concisely
COMMUNICATE your USP
ENGAGE with an open question
CLOSE for a follow up

Put it all together and practice it!

Try to keep a business card or other takeaway item with you which will help the other person remember you and your message.
Remember to cut out from your pitch any information that doesn't absolutely need to be there!

A summary of the key steps of the sale

I should remind all of us at this moment on our journey that for success we must keep in the forefront of our minds the need to structure our sale.

Let's just go back to basics for a moment to ensure that we have them firmly planted in our minds and that we will use the key steps *throughout the sale and each time, every time.*

Here is a short summary of the key steps to help us professionally manage a sale with a few helpful pointers at this stage.

Prospecting
Preparation
Planning
Presentation
Objection handling
Closing and follow up

Prospecting

We identify potential customers we might be able to help.

Preparation

We prepare before we engage a possible customer. We should research their business and their likely needs.

Planning

We determine how we can best help them with their need. We examine how our products or services will address their need.

Presentation

We carefully construct how we will present a solution.

Objection handling

We identify and isolate any real objection our prospect might still have.
We provide a solution to the concern and explore their approval.

Close and follow up

We take control, provide the best way forward, confirming the order, managing and influencing the sale.

Remember

Never miss a call back; always do what you say you will do; ensure your customer feels important; ensure you have provided the solution; ensure your customer feels you'll do your best.sIt is this strategy that will make you successful in your sales.

Building relationships

"The key to this business is personal relationships" from the film Jerry Maguire.

Tom Cruise in the film might have been referring to the business of sports representation in that classic movie, but sales professionals should take note of his advice.

The key to many successful partnerships throughout society is building quality relationships. We see that in successful marriages, sports, film stars, musicians and of course in business.

The sales industry is one that is largely built on relationships. If you want to generate repeat business with a client then it stands to reason that you have to first work on building a good relationship. Sometimes it can feel like you are wasting precious time engaging in conversation with a potential client, not being sure whether anything useful will come of it. Be patient and put the time into every conversation because you never know what it can lead to. Be ready to decide one way or the other on a prospect. Continually ask yourself this question: 'What are the chances of this leading to good business?'. I say 'Good business' because it's easy to chase after interested prospects who at the same time have no real need or intention of doing business with you.

I have been as guilty as anyone in being too quick to rush to judgement on a client's value to my business. There was a potential client who, once I had established a relationship with him, often engaged me in conversation about ideas for his business. He was developing a prototype product which he believed would eventually 'catch on', a product that would change the way we heat our homes and factories but the development had some way to go at that time and so he appeared to me as something of a workshop inventor. He would ring me regularly to discuss his progress and I was hesitant about the time I was spending speaking with him not sure that it was a good use of my time. Eventually he requested that I make a trip to see his factory in Northern Ireland and learn first hand about his products. I reluctantly agreed to make the journey thinking that it was time I would better spend achieving other sales. I arrived at quite a large factory which had significant investment, I toured the facility and met everyone there, had lunch and listened carefully throughout the day. As a result of my trip he became a key client for my Company and entrusted all his sales requirements to me. Incidentally, the new technology product he was developing was ground and air source heat pumps which are now gradually replacing traditional gas heating.

That was a valuable lesson to me in giving time to clients and listening carefully to their needs.

Whether you are a small business or a larger business with a dedicated prospecting team the key objective is to build quality relationships with your clients. As relationships grow directors of smaller organisations or the sales representatives of the larger companies need to focus on maintaining and improving those relationships.

To a large extent we use our own personality to establish good contact with clients but there needs to be a plan to develop a business relationship. This means that first of all we have to possess the qualities necessary to initiate the relationship and to forge a lasting bond with the client which becomes a profitable relationship between both organisations.

This is not always easy. You can be met with a reluctance at first to open up on the part of a decision maker. After all, they are charged with the responsibility of protecting and growing their business and they will be judged on the decisions they make.

The hardest part for the sales professional is to initiate the connection in the first place.

Never underestimate making even the slightest contact with a business professional. Always give time to see where a conversation can go. Some of the best business opportunities can come from showing a passing interest, a casual or even polite conversation or from making a helpful comment. We've all heard of the expression *'Right place; right time'*.

How do we start to build a relationship?

We all have to deal with annoying sales calls on a daily basis. They usually follow the same pattern. They call you by your first name from the outset and ask you how you are today with no real interest in your well being.

They have immediately created a barrier between themselves and their prospect.
They are unprepared for the call; no research or effort had been made to engage with you.
The first impression is poor and most likely will lead to an immediate rejection.

We have already seen that preparation for a call whether in person or on the telephone is key to your success. Part of your preparation has to be how you intend to establish a relationship with the decision maker.
Make sure that you know exactly who you are calling and what their role is in the Company. If you go into a

call without this information you can flounder and look stupid. This will not create a good impression at all.

When you start the conversation with the decision maker it is vital that you have prepared your call as follows:

Check that you are speaking to the correct decision maker
State clearly the reason for your call
Have a clear plan as to how you will sell the features, advantages and benefits of your products and services
Know how you want to close the call and what outcome you want to achieve

How do we know that we have identified the real decision maker?

Having prepared the call you have established the name and position of the decision maker.
You can't always be sure that this person will be the exact person you will need to speak with or that the person who deals with you is the same person.
How do we check?

'Mr Jones? Good morning Mr Jones! Good to speak with you. Are you the person responsible for the purchase of widget components?' 'Who else is involved in the decision?'

You are showing respect to the person you have identified as decision maker but you are also checking the route to the sales decision with an open question.

If you get a negative from Mr Jones then you can ask: *'Who do I need to be speaking to concerning this?'* And follow it up right away with: *'Is she in this morning?'*

This ensures that you make the most of your call.

How do we gain their confidence and put them at their ease?

There is a direct correlation between the preparation you made for your call, the way you professionally addressed the decision maker and their confidence in you.
Even the toughest decision maker would have to respect your approach to them. They may not 'crack' instantly but rest assured you will be well on the way to getting through to them.

Putting them at their ease is where your character comes into play!

You will need to establish small yet important connections between you such as:

Complementing them on their products or, in the circumstances of an appointment, their offices.

A question might be: how long they have worked for the organisation or, if they are the proprietor when they established the firm.

You may notice a trophy or a team affiliation on the wall and you make a personal connection.

These are subtle ice breakers which you will need to be aware of if you are to begin building a quality business relationship with you future client.

Keep your conversation relaxed but focused. It will be important for the decision maker to know that you don't waste time - neither his nor your own.

How do we get them to open up and give us information?

As you build your relationship never lose sight of your previously prepared objectives during your call.

As the decision maker begins to open up you can gradually and subtly feed in your questions to the conversation. People enjoy talking about themselves as a rule and the more encouraged they are the more open they become.

Always be honest.

After a while decision makers will realise your intention is to open up the conversation and to obtain information. This can occasionally cause them to close down the flow. Retrieval is still relatively easy by simply backing off slightly and confirming your intentions, such as:

'It has been a pleasure talking with you today. My only objective is to see whether there is a way we can work together which could be mutually beneficial. What are your thoughts?'

Such an approach, in an honest manner, usually results in taking the relationship to the next level. You will already have built enough confidence in the decision maker to continue to the next stage. If not, then you have to ask whether the prospect is still viable.

You will not do business with everyone and so take a timely view. The important thing is that you have tested it.

Messaging

As we have discussed, the sales industry is one that is largely built on relationships.

Our primary concern as we build a relationship with our client is that they understand the message we are there to convey.

Getting your message across

At the forefront of every business lies the desire to turn over profit, that's how businesses grow and flourish. But how exactly is this achieved? Sales is the answer.
The ultimate goal of every business, whether large or small, international or independent, is to make sales and make a profit. We all go out to work day to day to make our contribution to this common effort and share in the rewards.
But sales is surely about conveying a message?

Here, it would be useful to take a look at 'Messaging' in sales.

These days we are conveying and listening to messages all the time. Facebook, Instagram, Twitter and many more platforms are conveying instant messages all day long.
We send text messages and WhatsApp messages throughout each day. So messaging has become part of our 'everyday'.

During the recent Pandemic we have had many examples of messages being conveyed to the public. These have been both HARD messages and SOFT messages.
Here are some examples of HARD messaging:

'Stay at home'
'Wash hands'
'Protect the NHS'

Communicating a hard message isn't always easy for leaders to convey.
Hard messages must always convey the truth;
They must be clear and concise and to the point for the listener to grasp.
Space must be provided to allow the recipient to understand and respond.

The use of hard messages in a democratic country requires tact and diplomacy to achieve compliance, whereas in autocratic countries governments can simply 'tell' their populations and expect it.

Most Western countries depend on the consent of their population to accept hard messages when required but generally rely on influencing and eliciting a favourable response as we have experienced recently in the handling of issues related to the Covid crisis.

In contrast, a soft message elicits a positive and favourable response from the recipient.
It is low pressure, persuasive and encourages compliance.

Some examples of SOFT messaging:

'Stay safe'
'Try to work from home if you can'
'We're doing our best to keep you safe'

Similarly in sales we use hard and soft messaging all the time to sell our products and services.
So, a SOFT SELL approach uses subtle, encouraging and non-aggressive language. It depends on a more consultative approach, low pressure and persuasive techniques which do not always result in an immediate sale but helps to encourage a relationship and repeat orders.

Understanding a soft sell requires a sales person to use a subtle approach where the objective of the sale is no less important but the sale is not pushy.
The key is to build a relationship with the customer; allow the customer to relax and become confident in the products or services being offered.

The soft sell approach requires more energy and determination on the part of the sales person to build the relationship and keep the customer's interest. It requires regular reinforcement of the key features, the advantages and the benefits to the customer.

By contrast, the HARD SELL is designed to push the customer into buying in the short term. It relies on more aggressive techniques such as the fear of missing out, availability and peer pressures designed to achieve the sale immediately or within a short period of time.

For example: The sale must end today! Don't miss out!

We will examine soft or hard selling in more detail later in the programme in the section on the psychology of selling.

Language in selling

Associated with messaging comes the use of language and tone.

The language we choose to use is vital to our success in selling. We should think carefully how we convey our sales message and the language we use. We have only to think of the way we have been handled by sales people or customer services to see the importance of language in how we convey our message.

It can even be simply the tone used for our message:

'Stay on the line, your call is important to us'

Think about the different ways this message can be interpreted.

This message, put strongly and with concern, is conveyed with urgency and importance. It becomes a hard message to elicit compliance and suggests that it is in the listener's interest to stay on the line.

With different emphasis, the message can convey a very different interpretation. Your call may be treated as more of a nuisance. Just another call which has to be dealt with.

The question we have to ask when preparing to speak with a customer is:

'How do I convey my message to ensure that I take my customer with me?'

Understanding your buyer and their needs

Building a relationship with your prospective client helps you understand their needs and requirements.
This principle has been widely accepted and reflected in the development of online commerce.
We are now used to website cookies getting to know our preferences. If we search online for something we can find that adverts pop up on our future searches suggesting possibilities for purchase for some time afterwards.
Sales people have been building pictures of their clients well before the advent of the internet.
Algorithms on the internet now mimic the sales process.

Keys to understanding your customer

What are the key points of reference a sales person must employ to be able to understand a customer's needs and preferences?

Listen

If you give them the chance, your customer will tell you what they need.
Ask enough open questions and pay attention to your client's responses.

Only then can you offer a solution.

Give feedback

Find out whether your products or services fit with what your client is looking for.
See if there are any small adjustments you can make to find a better solution for them.
Be prepared to change, adapt or customise your offering to better fit their needs.

Interests

Find things that you have in common with your client so that you can develop a bond.
Ask about the things that they enjoy.
Share common interests.

Promptly

Be prompt in your response.
This shows the customer that they are your priority.
It demonstrates your sense of urgency on their behalf.
It is flattering for a customer to know that you attach so much importance to them.
Keeping in touch on progress for them ensures you remain in their mind.

Add value

Find ways to offer extra value to the relationship.
Provide a fresh perspective for them, an add-on for free, additional help or expertise.
Show that you want to work with them.

Conversations not sales pitches

When you are involved in a selling situation always engage your client in a conversation.
Keep it nice and relaxed.
Never feel the need to push.
You need to keep your focus on the relationship you are intending to build with the client.
At the same time, you can gradually and yet clearly explain the benefits to them.
Naturally move towards your sale.

Be genuine

People can feel sincerity.
They will know if you are being sincere. They will also know if you are simply interested in a sale!

Make your buyer's life easier

Put yourself in your clients shoes!
Make sure that your client enjoys working with you!
Make their life easier by finding solutions for them.
Get to know their timescale.
Help to make them look good.
Be available to your client whenever they might need you.

These relationship building methods work no matter what you are selling.

Psychology of sales

Psychology plays a very important part in selling.
Defined it is *'the study of human behaviour'*.
We will investigate the motivations and the triggers that are involved in a sale in the following chapters.

Specifically:

The psychology of the sales person
The psychology of the buyer and
The application of psychology for success in sales

The psychology of the sales person

Business generates the wealth in the country.
The people who achieve the sales are the most vital people in any business.

80 / 20 rule

Have you heard of the 80/20 rule?
This is a yardstick used in many business settings and is generally accurate.
80 percent of sales are achieved by the top 20 percent of sales people.
Why is this?
It could be explained by the small differences in ability and motivation which can lead to enormous differences in results.

80% of your sales will come from 20% of your customers
80% of your sales will come from 20% of your ad spend
20% of your prospects will give you 80% of your sales
80% of your success will come from 20% of your work
So, make every call count!
Remember from our earlier discussion to prepare well for your sale. Structure your sale - pay attention to detail and you will get the result you want!

The key psychological drivers of the sales person

It would be easy here to list the attributes of the perfect business person but I'm going to drill down to the essentials:

Self perception

A sales professional needs to know what he or she is capable of, what they really want from their career and how motivated they are to achieving their goals.

Do I have the capacity to be a high achiever?
Do I really want to be a high achiever?
Am I really prepared to put myself through the pain required to achieve my goals?

These are the serious questions that need to be faced at the outset if you want to be successful.
If the answer to any of the above is 'No' then there are other less stressful professions that could be a better option.

Fear of failure

We have all experienced the fear of failure at some time in our lives. Perhaps when were were awaiting exam results in school or university, or following a job interview.

In sales there is the fear of rejection which can become a mindset if not handled in your training.
There can be a genuine fear of picking up the 'phone and speaking with a decision maker.

What if they don't want to speak to me?
What if they just put the 'phone down?
What if they don't like my products?
What if they don't like ME?

Remember that at the beginning they don't even know you, they are unaware of the benefits you can bring to them.

What's the worst that can happen? They say 'No.' Once you have internalised these points you can overcome your fears and start to build the structure of handling a sales call.

Listening, empathy and relationship building

There is little point in pursuing a career in sales if you find empathy difficult or if it is something you don't enjoy.
Your first activity in sales is to use your ears. Listen carefully to your customer.

Sales is completely about building relationships and understanding the needs and requirements of other people.
Sales is all about understanding these needs and providing a solution.
It requires excellent listening skills, patience, creativity and flexibility.

Optimism

Are you a 'glass half full' or a 'glass half empty' type of character?
Sales people need to be always 'glass half full' in their dealings with their clients.

You have to believe you can find good customers.
Tenacity and the willingness to 'go the extra mile' will lead to success. For every *yes* you get, there will be eight to ten who say *no*.
Keep going and keep up the numbers. If you do, the numbers will look after you!
Believe you have products or services that will benefit your clients.

Know that you can provide solutions for your customers.
Sales has been described as a 'numbers game'. Put in the work and keep up the activity.
Ultimately, know you will be successful.

Creative

Being creative usually demands effort.
It means thinking up solutions to challenges that confront us.
It means making something happen - sometimes out of nothing.
It means putting in the time and your personal resources to find a sale when others might have given up.
It means resilience, being smart and caring enough to go the extra mile for your client.

Drive and motivation

Clearly linked to our last point - being creative - having the drive and
determination to succeed is fundamental to your sales success.

'Do I want it badly enough?'
'Am I prepared to put in the effort required for my success?'

We said that if you put in the numbers, the numbers will take care of you.
A motivated sales person will seize the opportunity, keep up the numbers, know what his or her conversation rate of prospects to buyers is. For example:

For every 10 prospective customers spoken to - 2 will buy which means a 1 in 5 conversion or 'success' rate.
We can also describe this as our 'efficiency rate'.
These are the basics necessary for your success. Make them part of your life and any fears associated with your sales success will subside.

Responsibility, accountability and self discipline

In all walks of life we have responsibility, accountability and we need self-discipline if we are to achieve the goals and the success we desire. Similarly in sales we have to put in the effort to get the results. There is no easy or quick fix and we don't rely on luck. I remember a comment made to me many years ago 'You make your own luck' in sales.

As a young inexperienced sales person my Managing Director joined one day as I was making calls to prospective clients. As he observed me working he made this comment:
'You need to be more greedy!'
I instantly understood from his comment that I lacked sufficient tenacity. I knew that I needed more persistence in my dealings with clients, my desire for a successful outcome and personal gain.
I remembered his comment throughout my professional career.

I soon realised that sales is a numbers game.

You have to put in the calls, make the effort.
With every call I made I was one call closer to a 'Yes' from a client.
This is the discipline required of a successful sales person and there is no easy way.

Confidence

When you are new to sales and full of ambition the natural reaction is to think that the sky's the limit. But as the weeks go by and the effort goes in the dream can fade a little.
A streak of rejections can knock the confidence of the most driven sales person.
The faith and optimism of the beginner can be crowded out by fear, pessimism and self-doubt.

You have just begun. You are on a journey.
If you really believe in yourself and you can muster a 'can-do' attitude then, once you master the basics, your fears will subside and you will become successful.

Goals and objectives driven

The most successful sales people are the ones who can see themselves sailing past the finish line, winning the race.
The most successful sales people know that they have it within themselves to win, to be the best.
This is not conceit, smugness or presumption.

This is a quiet confidence that if I apply myself, if I learn and if I am determined then I *will* succeed.

Always visualise the outcomes you want:

To end the year as the best sales person in the team
To achieve a turnover figure you have projected
To build your business to a target level this year

Then you can visualise the rewards you are looking for:

To achieve the bonus earnings you have projected for yourself
To buy the car, the house or other goal you long for
To reach a personal objective or the promotion you strive for.

What makes a good sales person or a bad sales person?

At the end of my first year as manager of my first sales team, Company results were published which showed that my operation was the most successful in the business at year end.
The Managing Director came to visit me soon after and asked me this question:

'Why are you the most successful profit centre in the Company?'

My reply didn't go down too well. This was during the 80's. A time when hard nosed and flamboyant sales characters seemed to be admired. But times were changing.

I asked in reply 'Would you be surprised if I told you that my team are not the hardest sales people in the Company?' He looked bemused and without comment left my office.

The point I probably failed to make was that my team were more focused on building relationships and fact finding exactly the needs of the customer rather than pushing relentlessly for the next sale. This was a significant change in those days and it was indicative of the way sales would change in the coming years.

We have all had some experience of both the good sales person and the bad one. It's probably the bad one that we remember the most, the one who talks without listening, have only their own objectives in mind, keen to get a sale at any cost.

Think about an experience where you have benefited from a good sales person, the one who listened carefully to your requirements, who made helpful suggestions, who didn't push you, the one for whom you put up good reviews online.

We can have a quick look at both the good qualities and the bad ones just to show the difference.

The good sales person

'Every day is full of opportunities and I can build my pipeline of possibilities'.
If you approach each day with this positive self-view then prospecting will not be a problem for you.

So, why do we do it at all?
We all go to work to earn money and we have to believe in our success.

A sales person should consider the following questions:

Do you see yourself as a £25,000 a year person or a £75,000 a year person?
Do I have personal or family goals I want to achieve?
How and when do I want to achieve them?

If you take steps to challenge your self-limiting beliefs you'll boost your self-esteem and your sales performance. Successful sales people are in control of their 'inner-dialogues'. A successful sales person thinks successful thoughts.

We are going to look at key indicators for the sales person's success later in this chapter.

The bad sales person

This person will look for short cuts to get a deal.
Faced with the tough task of many prospecting calls this person will try to cut corners and persuade customers with false promises.
The bad sales person will not see integrity as important in their approach.
They will not put value on building good relationships with customers. They have no interest to provide the best outcome for their customer.

The bad sales person will try to maximise their income by whatever means.
They will not enjoy their role and they will not achieve long term success.

The benefits of being a good sales person

The benefits of great relationships with quality people
Enhanced communication skills
Personal development both professional and social
Greater negotiating powers
Growth in self confidence

A tougher and more mature outlook on life generally
Capability to rise to new challenges
Self discipline and persistence
Enhanced earning potential
Great prospects

Key personal indicators for sales success

Goals and ambitions

What do I want to achieve?

Do I set annual income goals?
How much do I want to earn?
How much can I earn?

How do I achieve my goals?

Do I set annual sales targets?
What did I target last year?
What will I target this year?
Did I achieve my sales target last year?

Break down the task into manageable chunks.
Managing activity and productivity

Break down the sales activity task into weekly and monthly goals

Each day, come in and set the daily target you need to achieve
Focus daily on activity required, calls, appointments to help achieve your targets

Important

Never allow yourself to under achieve with your activity. You are the only person who will lose out if you give yourself an excuse.

Personal confidence

Confidence isn't a skill you can be taught in the way you can learn to sell.
Rather it is a state of mind.
How confident are you as a person in your personal life? In your professional life?

Think about the most confident person you know for a moment.
Why are they so confident?
Is it due to their upbringing?
Successful parents?
Wealth or education?
How do you compare to them?

Fear factor

Let's consider for a moment the qualities you will need for your confidence:
Positive thinking
'Can-do' attitude
Knowledge and training
Experience
Belief in your ability

Characteristics to avoid at all costs:

Fear of failure - which will only fill the void of a lack of planning or preparation
Stress - which again will be overcome by your knowledge and planning Arrogance - if you don't put your client's needs first

Ways to improve your confidence in sales

Preparation
Know what you have to offer and how to present it planning or each call or meeting
Cover the angles
The customer's needs or concerns
Practice
Rehearse your sales call with colleagues, project yourself with confidence

Professional
Dress confidently and appropriately for your meeting
Control the situation
Manage the meeting and break down the tasks
Contingency plans
Cover the 'what ifs' ahead of any sales meeting

In many ways, much of the above comes down to your planning, preparation and organisation. If you have put in the effort ahead of your sales call you will have established sufficient confidence to handle any situation that may arise.

Sales is like going into battle knowing that you must win,

we prepare for every eventuality
we cover all the angles
we have a plan we know we will achieve our objectives

How impressed we are when we hear the comment that someone is 'On top of their game'.

Now we know why!

Using psychology for sales

How do we apply the psychology we have been considering to the basics of selling?

Identifying a decision maker

We have learned that thorough preparation before making contact with a prospective Company is essential if you hope to have any success in sales.

Remind yourself of the basic plan

Researching the products and services of the company.
Understanding their management structure and identifying who are the likely decision makers.
This may depend on the size of the company, its organisational structure and likely markets.

Do not underestimate the power of the company gatekeeper - the receptionist or secretary who answers the telephone. This person can be a vital source of information well before you get through to the decision maker, so build a relationship to obtain useful 'insider' information.

Information you need to find

Who is responsible for purchasing products like yours?
Who else is involved? managing director, product manager, buyer manager, etc.

Build a picture of the how things are organised

Which day is the decision maker usually in the office?
What is the best time to catch him?
You will need to build something of a relationship with the 'Gatekeeper' to find out this information.
Again, do not underestimate their influence in the company.
The director is likely to ask what they think of you and your approach towards them.

How to manage the first meeting with a new decision maker

Let us imagine that you have been given an opportunity to meet with a proposed decision maker. How do I handle this first encounter:

First impressions are key.
Be concise and well organised. Identify their needs rather than focus on your own.
Listen for 'buying signals' which indicate their desire, likely competition, need, and other triggers.
Control the meeting - time, objective and likely outcome. Ensure you have a clear exit strategy with options.

First impressions are vital to both the continuation of the meeting and your ultimate success.

You get one bite of the cherry - one chance to make an impression and the decision maker will sum up in the first minute whether he wants to do business with you or not.

Relationship is the most basic and advantageous outcome at this point.

How NOT to conduct a sale

An Illustration

I'm reminded of an old training video where a pushy sales person enters a potential customer's office.
He says ' Hi, Geoff! You don't mind me calling you Geoff..
Without waiting for a response he continues:
'Geoff, Have I got a deal for you! This is going to blow your mind.' 'Geoff ' in the meantime is trying to get a word in but doesn't manage it.

The sales person continues without a breath 'You sign up for these products today and I'll give you 50% off! No Geoff. You're my kind of guy. Let me ring my manager and see if we can do an even better deal. Wait.'
He immediately turns and rings his manager. As he comes off the 'phone he turns and says:
'Geoff, I'm going to give you and extra 10% on top of my original deal..What do you you say about that? Only today Geoff! I can't hold off. It's today only Geoff. Great Stuff!!'

'Let's get this paperwork signed off and I'll be away'. He passes the paperwork over, bids Geoff a great day and leaves.
Geoff, still a bit dumbstruck, picks up the 'phone on his desk to make an internal call:

'Hi, it's Colin here from accounts. I've just had the weirdest guy in my office calling me Geoff. I've no idea what he wanted.'

What just happened here?

He hadn't prepared
He didn't know who the decision maker was
He assumed everything
His introduction was poor and didn't build a relationship

He has no chance of a sale

The consequences of being unprepared

Let's take a look now at the consequences of being unprepared when attempting to conduct a sale.
In times gone by, sales representatives were encouraged to 'call in' to speculatively create sales when they are in an area. I would discourage any effort to create a sale on this basis alone.

So, let's imagine another scenario…

An Illustration

A widget salesman sees a potential prospect company whilst on an industrial estate and decides to make a cold call.

He convinces the receptionist to find out whether the 'buyer' will give him a few minutes of her time.

He is directed to the buyer's office and knocks on the door.

The buyer bids him to come in. He enters saying: 'Thank you so much for seeing me today' and then promptly sits at the desk without first being asked.

He launches into his pitch, noticing the buyer's name on the desk, forgetting formality he says: 'So, Lauren, can I call you Lauren? How's it going?

Not waiting for a response, he put his briefcase on her desk and pulled out a sample widget, the latest model his company is producing.

'Wait 'till you see this latest model. You'll love it!' He sits back in his chair, pulls out a pack of gums and offers her one. She politely refuses. He says:

'You don't mind if I do?' Not expecting a response.

'OK' continues the salesman, 'I know that these little beauties will be excellent for your production. I can do these at rock bottom prices for you, provided we do a deal today'.

The buyer politely examines the widget and places it on the table.

The salesman, thinking that he's doing a great job and is in with a shout of a sale, changes the subject to the weather. 'Lovely day out there today, isn't it'.

Returning to the subject of the sale he persists: 'So, let's write up an order for say 50 and see how it goes.' The buyer, who has clearly had enough stands up and starts to end the conversation.

The salesman, realising that it's now or never, stands too and reiterates his offer of a reduction that day only. She says 'I'll discuss it with the production manager and we'll be in touch'. Realising he is losing his chance of a sale, he switches his close: 'I'll call you in a day or so and find out when you want to go ahead'.
The buyer bids him 'Good day' and he leaves without his sale.

What just happened here?

He turned up without any preparation
He cold called a prospective customer
He talked his way into seeing a buyer, not knowing whether she was the real decision maker
He was too familiar, unprofessional and made no attempt to either recognise the position of the buyer or her role
He sat down uninvited, invaded the space on her desk
He didn't enquire as to her interest in seeing his company product
He made assumptions that their company would benefit from this particular widget
He failed to pick up on either buying signals or lack of them from the buyer

He would not have identified any body language being given off by the buyer either
Again, he assumed that the buyer would be interested in a one-time offer but
Had not established who the real decision maker would be He started to lose control of the so-called 'meeting
He had not gained any knowledge of the buying process ...and most of all, He had not established any kind of relationship

This call was going nowhere and no sale was on the horizon.

In both these rather amusing illustrations we can see how both people lacked the most elementary understanding of the selling process. Unfortunately, there are still companies today who fail to equip their sales people with basic skills for selling and lack any sales structure when dealing with clients.

Professional selling

The sales person's function has changed immeasurably in recent years and is currently undergoing further change as a result of the Pandemic and the ensuing economic situation.

The days of cold calling are behind us and in its place a new professionalism is required.

Whilst a physical presence in a region can be an advantage in the sense that a prospecting sales person can see opportunities that might be of interest, they now have the added advantage of immediate research online.
There is no excuse for not researching or being unprepared these days.

We can still build the best kind of relationship by meeting in person but events recently have inspired new modes of communication. We are now comfortable meeting on Zoom or Microsoft Teams which are good and acceptable forums for doing business. These new ways have other benefits such as people being able to work from home, much reduced need for travel to clients or to the office.

No matter how sophisticated we become or how much technology we are able to rely upon, the basic principles of selling remain the same and will never change.

A sales professional must research a prospective customer carefully. Generally there is no shortage of information available to build a significant picture of a prospect.

The information required to prospect a potential client now should be:

Finding out the key decision makers and their contact information
A clear understanding of the company products and services
Who their customers are likely to be
To identify just how your company and its products and services might be of interest to them

From this information you can build your sale and plan how to present it to them.
You will be able to identify their likely concerns about your products or the likely costs.

The key thing about selling is building a quality business relationship with your prospect.
So, its going to be vital that you have thought through exactly how your products and services might benefit this prospective client.

We could not have imagined trading conditions like the ones we are now facing as a result of the Pandemic. This means that you must build a better quality relationship with these prospectives than others who compete with you. You must have more to offer than your competitors and you must be prepared to go the extra mile for them to provide solutions.

The quality of relationship you build will determine just how much ongoing business you can achieve from each client.
If you can do this then you will hopefully be able to compete successfully for the smaller volume of business potential that is currently available.

This is how your business will compete and ultimately survive.

Creating a sense of urgency tactfully

Remember we said that building a relationship with our customer is key. It helps us understand the client and their needs.

Algorithms and website cookies are being deployed all day and every day in our lives to understand our buying habits.

They are pervasive in every aspect of our online life, getting to know our preferences.
For example, if you 'Google' something one day, before you know it adverts are popping up every time you search the internet for the products you were looking for earlier.

Good quality sales professionals have been building pictures of their clients' preferences well before the advent of the internet.

Algorithms on the internet now mimic the sales process.

Algorithms are useful but they aren't tactful.

Human beings have a huge advantage here!

We can identify the *best moment* to suggest, encourage or lead our prospect towards the purchase. However, we can only do this with the careful use of two factors:

Relationship
Knowledge

Good relationships help you understand your clients and their needs.

In the same way as websites collect 'cookies' and information on visitors to get to know their preferences, sales people collect information to build their knowledge of their clients.

This has been the way sales people have worked since way before the days of the internet.

Using language effectively to influence our listener

We all have to decide how we use language for our sales. Sometimes we don't realise that we are choosing our language but we are!
Remember how we have discussed hard and soft use of language? Psychology plays a role here in how we influence our listener.

There is an expression: 'Sell rather than tell'
It is hugely important which method we choose to convey our message. Let's look at some examples that we have all experienced recently: Here's a good example of a hard message:

'We will be leaving the EU on the 31st of December, do or die!' That's 'telling'.

Take this one - an example of a soft message:

'I think it would be important to take the decision back for a confirmatory vote'
This could be an appeal or be seen to be selling the idea to the listener.

So we have a choice in the way we convey information and influence our listener:

Tell
We instruct that this is how it is
Sell

Give advantages and benefits so the listener will comply
Appeal
We ask for their support giving good reasons
Illicit
We get them to come up with the idea themselves
Encourage
We motivate them into an affirmative position

Choosing our words

Does choosing certain words improve the communication of our message?

Choosing the right words to convey our message in sales is vitally important.
It not only creates an impression of the sales person conveying the message but it can determine whether the message itself is important or not.

In sales there is a time for conveying hard messages and a time for conveying soft messages.

Take these two examples:

'It's hugely important that you act now to ensure delivery on time'
Hard message
'I would really recommend this product for your application'
Soft message

Both provide a solution to the benefit of the customer and both have the capacity to illicit a favourable response from the customer.

Examples of words conveying a *hard* message: *'*

Imperative'
'Hugely important'
'Vital'
Examples of words conveying a *soft* message

'Ideal'
'Advisable'
'Desirable'

Exercises to try:

Think of examples of words you could use to put over a hard message. Think of examples of words you could use to put over a soft message. Think of how we use words to 'take people with us' - to convince them.

Words are a hugely important tool and they need to be crafted carefully.

Understanding your customer

'The grass is always greener on the other side'.

We often hear this quoted by people who feel that life could be better or their chances might need an uplift. But I want to use this well-worn saying in an entirely different context - for selling. The best sales person will go well beyond fact finding the needs of their client and then making an attempt to address them. The best sales person will try to stand with their client, on their grass, and take in the view that their client sees or wishes to see. The best sales person is not someone who looks at the client but looks in the *same direction* as their client - sees what they see; can see the possibilities that they envisage. If the sales person can achieve that vantage point then they have gone a long way to understanding their client, their needs and requirements.

Relationship building

I would go so far as to say the most important aspect of selling is relationship building.

Whilst it has always been the bedrock of commercial activity, in recent years the building of quality relationships has become fundamental to quality salesmanship. Decision makers appreciate the sales person who can provide a solution, who cares about their organisation and them personally. They appreciate a relationship built upon honesty and trust. They are human beings who will appreciate a friendly contact and someone who can listen.

Why should I put emphasis on relationships?

It is impossible to provide answers or solutions to your client's needs if you don't know what they need.
It is impossible to find out their needs unless you have put time into building a relationship or trust enabling your client to open up about their needs.

How do I build a relationship?

There are 5 key components to making this happen:

Listening

If you are a good listener your customers will tell you what they need if you give them the chance. Ask quality OPEN questions to illicit the information you still need. Only then can you offer a solution.

Feedback

Find out if your product fits what your clients are looking for. Determine how flexible you can be to provide a solution that fits. See if there are any adjustments you can make to find a better solution. The happier they are the more likely the sale.

Interest

Show genuine interest in the decision maker. Look for things that you have in common with your client so that you can develop a bond. Encourage them to talk about their time in the business. Ask about the things that they enjoy and share common interests.

Prompt action

Act promptly on behalf of your client. This shows that you regard them as your priority.
It is flattering for a customer to know that you attach so much importance to them.
Keeping in touch about your progress on their behalf keeps you in their mind and can allow for arranged return calls to progress your sales.

Going the extra mile

This will ensure that you build a quality relationship. Here are 4 more points to go the extra mile:

Add value

Find ways to offer added value to the relationship; a fresh perspective, an add-on for free, additional help or expertise. Providing knowledge which in turn adds authority and gravitas. It demonstrates that you want to work with them.

Conversation

Keep your conversations relaxed and don't be pushy. Again this will add to your authority and gravitas. It will help you keep your focus on the relationship whilst ensuring the benefits are clearly explained. Move comfortably towards your sale.

Genuine

Being approachable and always honest with your client will be the basis for a long term relationship. People can feel sincerity and at first they will be cautious until they feel that they can trust you. Decision makers also know when a sales person is simply interested in a sale. Remember that people buy from people they like.

Make life easier

A key part of achieving business with a client is to make their life easier for them. Be helpful, find solutions for their needs. Help them to look good! If

you make their life easier by finding good solutions which makes them look good you will develop repeat business with those clients.
Be available at all times.

Structure your sales activity

In building a good relationship with your client you need to be sure to use use quality and structured sales techniques to achieve your sale. There's absolutely no point in building the best relationships possible and yet never achieving your sales!

Refining the sales process

Whilst the *key points* of the sale must remain the absolute focus of the sales process, there are some important ways to refine and complement the sales process.
So, at this point, I am going to first of all list the ways to refine the sales process and then remind you of the key steps of the sale.
I make no apology once again for refreshing your memory of these vital steps.

Key points to *refine* the sales process

Locating the decision maker
A quality presentation
Using narrative

Establishing a relationship
Understanding your client - needs and preferences
Listening skills
Feed back to the client
Sharing common interests

Key *steps* of the sale

Identify the decision maker
Present your product
Create urgency Isolate and handle any objections
Close the sale

Best practice for sales success

Everyone in business wants to know:

What is the key to be sure to achieve the sale? The first thing to say is that you won't get every deal going. The second is that, with the right approach and the right disposition, you can achieve almost every sale that is available. I'm going to give you the formula to your success in sales.

Conversation

You must initiate a genuine conversation and begin the task of building a relationship.
This can be quite tricky at first. Decision makers tend to be busy with little time for chat.
Their own consciousness of time management won't allow them to just 'pass the time of day'.
You have to acknowledge this in your earliest conversation.

Useful openers such as:

'I realise you are busy, I will only take a few minutes of your time' *'I appreciate you giving me a few minutes of your precious time'*

This way you are acknowledging his time is valuable and preventing him from telling you the same thing and closing down the conversation.

Engage

Engage with your customer. Get into his shoes a little.

Useful questions like:
'How's business for you at the moment?'
Or more recently:
'Have you been badly affected by the Pandemic downturn?'

Get the conversation wheels turning. React to the answers in an attuned way.

'Really?', *'Not easy at the moment'* and so on.

Now, at this point you have established the beginnings of a relationship and you have, even temporarily, gained the attention of your potential customer.

Build a quality relationship

Remember that people buy from people they like!
As you progress with your customer the key to your success is to continue to build a genuine relationship.
You must first make a personal connection with the decision maker so that they are motivated to engage with you.
As you fact find you will start to address their needs.

Offer solutions

Begin to offer solutions in a timely way:
'Right, I'm sure we can help with that. What I'm going to do is..'

Provide a plan and put it in a timescale that is suitable to your potential customer.
Make sure the customer understands that you are going to do the work.

Next, verify the plan and the timescale that suits your customer:

*'I'll see what I can come up with in the next few days and then I can come and see you.
What are your thoughts about having a short meeting next Tuesday morning, say at 11am?'*

You have built the relationship quickly and sufficiently to gain some trust from your potential customer for the following:

They agree to give you the scope to try to find a solution
They agree to meet the following week to discuss your progress

This is a significant achievement already.

Make their life easier

Most people like to think that their life could be a bit easier.
This is exactly the case in sales and in any business.
If your customer thinks that working with you will achieve this, you're already half way to your sale.
Make sure your client enjoys working with you.
Make their life easier. Find a solution for them.
Help them look good to their boss or colleagues.
Be available at all times so that they know you are just at the end of a 'phone for help.

Summary of key sales initiatives

You have opened a conversation with the decision maker
You have established communication with them
You have built a genuine dialogue with an element of trust
You have their agreement to try to find a solution for them
You agree to meet to discuss options

A great start to your sale!

Summary of the key steps of a sale

One final reminder!

Identify the decision maker
Present your product
Create urgency
Isolate and handle any objections
Close the sale

Identify the genuine decision maker

We have been discussing the importance of building a genuine relationship with the decision maker. Remember at this point to be absolutely sure you have identified the *genuine* decision maker.

There's no point in having the best relationship in the world with someone in the organisation who is happy to talk with you if that person is not the real decision maker - the person who signs the cheque!
What if you are facing a group of people, two perhaps, or more?
Identify which one is the decision maker and focus your attention and tactics towards that person.
If you gently press with a question as to who makes the decision you will generally get an honest answer.

'Who is involved in the decision?'
'Who else needs to be consulted before we can go ahead?'

Presentation of your products and services

Be enthusiastic about your products or your services!
If you aren't then you can't expect your customer to be enthusiastic. The last four letters of enthusIASM create an acronym - I AM SOLD MYSELF
If you are - they will be too!

Remember! What is your UNIQUE SELLING POINT? What are you offering that your competitor isn't able to offer? You need to up-sell this point.
It might be your competitive price, the quality you can offer, the quantity you can provide, the availability.
Be concise!

Create urgency

Everything sells at some point.
Similarly, people will decide to buy at some point during the process.
If you push too hard you can lose the opportunity; if you hesitate and wait someone else will get there before you!
Your relationship with the decision maker and their trust in you will be all important at this stage.
So, creating a sense of urgency really does help and you can do this in a 'non-pushy' way.
You may say:

'This particular product is in high demand at the moment. I can't guarantee they'll be here in a few days time.' and/or
'We've had a great deal of interest in this and I'm sure it will sell very quickly'.
Be tactful!

Use narrative

Tell your prospective customer how thrilled a previous customer was with this product and how you've built a great relationship with them. Show examples of how your products have improved the customer's results. This way you are more likely to achieve the sale.

Handle any objections

Oh no! There's a problem!
You might be tempted to think of a customer objection as a rejection. No, it really isn't the end of the world! Think of it this way - if a customer takes the time to tell you what his problem is:

'Its too expensive'
'I'm not sure about the quality'
'I've seen something else I like' The customer wouldn't go to the bother of telling you if it was a simple 'No'.
If a customer highlights a concern then surely it must be a 'buying signal'.

It might simply be a lack of information,
a fair concern such as price or
a perception issue, or
it can be a hidden objection such as a preferred supplier, or

it could be my lack of knowledge about their priorities this year.

If a customer is giving you the opportunity to address a concern - say *'Thank you!'* - it's good news!
First, make sure you empathise with the customer's viewpoint and concerns.

Qualify the concern

Qualify your client's needs to ensure you have understood correctly. Ask, probe and confirm to ensure that you have identified their real concerns and addressed them.

Isolate the key objection

'So then, are you saying that the only reason you are unsure about going ahead is…'
Price / delivery or whatever you have found out.
This should isolate the real objection and allows you to provide a solution.

Reconfirm the value of your offer to them.

Back it up with customer references, again use a narrative, a story of a happy customer.

You can then *overcome their concern* and move to close the sale.

Close for the sale

Once the customer is engaged with your product and the sale, progressing to the close should be relatively straight forward.

Options to close a sale

1. Direct close

'So, what are your thoughts on going ahead with the order?' You are asking a direct and open question to the customer. This enables the decision maker to decide on their terms not yours.

2. Assumptive close

'All we need to do now is to complete the order form and we'll get everything organised.' This is an easy way for the decision maker to go ahead without having to face up to a decision.

3. Alternative close

'So are you going to go for product A or product B?' - It's a choice of either/or.

4. Reverse close

'So, is there anything that would stop you from signing the order today?' - if no, you've got a deal.

5. Deferred close*

If you have to! Something like: 'So, you've said you like what you see today and there's no reason not to go ahead. We'll discuss the details or purchase, implementation and dates.' The deal is there for a later date.

*This one is not my preferred option because you are risking someone else moving in and getting the order or the decision maker changing their mind.

Reminder

80/20 rule

It it always worth remembering the 80/20 rule in business

80% of your sales will come from 20% of your customers
20% of your prospects will give you 80% of your sales
80% of your sales will come from 20% of your ad spend
80% of your success will come from 20% of your work

So make every call count. Structure your sale, pay attention to detail and it will pay off.

Customer services

I like to think that when I need information or help with a product or service there will be someone available to me either on the telephone or in response to an email enquiry that can assist me and provide reassurance. Most companies are too big for the owner to deal with every enquiry so they must delegate this important task to someone else. To be clear, when we need to address an enquiry or a concern to a company we should be dealing with the owners' representative - it's that important! This means that we would expect our enquiry to be handled efficiently, enthusiastically, clearly and most importantly to our satisfaction.

Customer service isn't a department; it's an attitude

It would be a mistake to regard 'Customer service' as a 'Department'. Customer service is exactly that 'providing a service to the customer'.

The whole concept of customer service has come into sharp focus in recent years, especially since the commercial crash of 2008.

All Companies both business to business and retail have realised that there are a limited amount of sales opportunities and only the best performers will survive.

As we face an even more severe test since the events of 2020 this will mean that only the very best will make it. So, our ability to satisfy our customer's needs is of the greatest importance.

Let's take a few examples of customer service we have all experienced recently.
I think we will learn that there are many ways we can improve our customer's experience.

Customer services on the telephone

We need to call 'Customer services' on the telephone. We dial the number, going through several options and before we ever get to speak to someone we experience the inevitable recorded message, usually:

'Your call is important to us. Please stay on the line. Your call will be answered shortly'

So we wait. Whilst we hang in there we are usually reminded again that our call is important.

Is that so? If it was really important someone would have answered!

Then we get the next message:

'We are experiencing a high level of calls, your call is in a queue'.

Then finally we are told:

'All our calls are recorded for training purposes'.

As customers how should we feel when we finally get through to the customer services representative?
Grateful that we have finally been answered? Understanding of the pressures on our services provider?

Absolutely not.
We are the customer and we should be far more important than their operational issues.
Instead, we will by now have the view that:

They are poorly staffed, cutting costs
They don't really mean that my call is important otherwise they would have answered right away
I don't need to know about their high call rate or capability issues

Remember we were informed that *'Calls are recorded for training purposes?'*

So, when we get through to someone, we'd fully expect a well trained customer services person to handle our enquiry?

'How can I help?'
Followed by:
'I'll put you through to someone who can take your call'.

What happened to the well trained person?
How are they doing so far?

So we find ourselves explaining the reason for our call twice over to people who are supposed to be 'well trained' according to the recorded message.

The customer is beginning to form the opinion that the company is incompetent.

Many companies both large and small expect far too much understanding from their customers.
If they just stop and consider how badly they are managing their customer so far, and up to this point they haven't even arrived at dealing with the enquiry, retaining their confidence has become almost impossible.

Keeping your customers waiting

Keeping your customer waiting is discourteous and destroys the confidence you are trying to build with them.

If you keep your client waiting without reason or apology you will have an uphill struggle to manage the meeting with them afterwards since you will have squandered any goodwill you had built previously.

If you have planned an appointment for your customer you must see them at that time.
This shows that you are organised and on top of your job.

If you have a pressing issue that must be dealt with before attending to your customer then have the courtesy to inform them and ask their permission. Inform them how long this issue will take so that they know the extent of the delay.

'No problem'

Recently dealing with the customer services department of a company I was being attended to by someone who, on repeated occasions, kept informing me that what she was doing for me was *'not a problem'*.

This is a curious thing to say to a customer. It suggests that there could be circumstances where providing customer services 'might' be a problem but on this occasion it wasn't.

To the customer, receiving confirmation that each aspect of providing a service to me hasn't been a problem suggests that they might normally see the customer as a problem but in this case they haven't.
Don't say it.

'Do this for me ...'

Another anomaly has crept into customer services in recent times and it can be found everywhere!

'Take a seat *for me*' - Reception
'Open your mouth *for me*' - Nurse
'Put these on *for me*' - Optician

Why would you request your customer to do something *for you*?
You are there to provide a service so it is you who should be doing things *for the customer*.
Please get rid of requests that make demands on your customer to do things for *you* and encourage customers *to do things for their benefit*.

Simply loose the '*for me*' and you will have corrected and improved your relationship with your customer hugely.

'Please take a seat'
'Can you open your mouth?'
'Try these on and see how they look'

Customer services for selling or problem handling?

Telecoms companies are some of the worst offenders. Inherently they provide poor services, charge over the odds and make significant profits.
The customer already realises this so they are already starting at a disadvantage in the call.

I have observed that if you call to speak to someone regarding a purchase they will be on the ball, careful to listen, the operative will be well sales trained and articulate.
On the other hand, if your call concerns fixing a problem or some other aspect of your existing contract you will usually be directed to a lengthy call waiting situation, and eventually end up speaking to

someone poorly trained and less able to provide a suitable response.

This is not providing any kind of acceptable service to the customer.

Companies that have outsourced their call-centre operations to other countries to cut their costs really need to examine whether their cost cutting outweighs their need to provide a good service to the customer.
In my experience, the better the customer experience - the more the profit.

Key points to ensure quality customer services

Don't keep your customer waiting
Don't patronise your customers with messages that their call is important - they know it is!
Don't explain that you have a large number of calls - your customer won't be interested
If you tell customers that you record calls for training purposes then your customer service representative needs to show their training and provide a quality response
Don't ask your customer to do something for you

Ensure that the only person who matters is your customer

Ensure that you understand what your customer needs, address those needs carefully, check that the customer is satisfied

Prompt action

There is a huge premium to be achieved by companies that act promptly to a customer request.

It's not rocket science; if you look after your customer's needs promptly and provide a solution to their need rapidly, the customer will be impressed and they will buy from you again.

If you keep a customer waiting you are sending out the message that the customer is not a priority, is less important and that their money is more important than they are.

Acting promptly shows the customer that *they* are your priority.

It is flattering for a customer to know that you attach so much importance to them.

Keeping in touch on your progress ensures good communication and develops the relationship.

Add value

Find ways to offer extra value to the relationship.
Give a fresh perspective to the customer, provide an add-on for free, give additional help or expertise.
Show that you *want* to work with them.
Go above and beyond for your customer. Make them feel that they are important and that you are going 'the extra mile' for them.
Again, you will help to build your relationship with them and they will come back to you rather than go to your competitor the next time they have a need.
This is just as important in customer services as it is in sales.

Writing to your clients

There are circumstances when it can be useful to write to your clients but I would always advise personal contact where possible. There have been significant changes in the way we communicate with customers over the years. Whilst the telephone has always been there, we remember the advent of the fax machine and the word processor which were forerunners of our modern day computers with online capability to communicate.

A word of caution to the sales person here. Using email, letters or other methods of communication rather than picking up the 'phone can be a cop out. It can be an excuse not to deal with the customer directly which could be perceived as a more difficult task.

There are statistics to consider here. If you opt for email communication with your clients be aware that less than eight percent of emails are actually opened and read. If you send mail to your client the real decision maker may never actually read it and your letter may easily be regarded as a sales mail shot and end up in the bin beside the desk.

There are opportunities that you can create by writing to your client on occasion. But I do stress that it should be for specific reasons.

I am reminded of an excellent email letter I received from the Managing Director and owner of a Company where I have purchased products previously.

He was writing to his clients during the Pandemic which created a good opportunity to reach out to them. He began the letter simply with 'Thank you'.
His next point was to reiterate that the Company was still available to provide services to their customers

with some details of necessary changes. This was useful and relevant information for me to keep reading. His next paragraph returned to a more personal note identifying with the many problems people have experienced in recent months which helped to reconfirm the relationship he had built with his customers.

He acknowledged that they may not have always been successful nor appreciative of their customers' patience. He reiterated the effort his team put in to support their 'amazing clients'. Comments such as these affirm the relationship with the customer.

This letter, although triggered by recent circumstances, is a good example of how a company can reach out to their clients through written communication.

Sales interview success

Interview success for sales professionals

Whilst there are many hints and tips available for interviews, sales professionals should consider specialist advice as to how they can be successful in the sales interview process.

I am the founder of an international sales recruitment organisation with many years of experience in this specialist market and I'd like to share my thoughts on sales interview success. One of the key formulas for the success of sales candidates who passed through our organisation was the benefit of interview training which I initiated in my own Company.

We wanted to make sure that our candidates created the best impression and gave themselves the best chance of securing the job they were applying for. This both improved our success rate and our reputation for putting forward the best available candidates. We formulated the procedure of candidate preparation so that our consultants made it part of their routine activity when handling applicants.

I want to pass on to you this formula so that, if you are applying for a sales position or indeed any other role, you too will benefit from being better prepared than any of your competitors.

Preparation for a sales interview

In the past I have been surprised by how little preparation some candidates have done to prepare for interview. Some candidates see their preparation as little more than putting together a Curriculum Vitae and looking at their prospective employers website ahead of the interview.

So, let's start at the beginning of the process.

The Curriculum vitae

It is customary to prepare a CV if you wish to apply for a position. The purpose of this is to provide the background information and experience of the applicant. The CV is really a clearing tool for employers to sift through the candidates and to make a decision as to whether there are any suitable applicants to call for interview.

This means that the CV is your first opportunity to sell yourself to a prospective employer. Candidates often forget this fact and put together a CV which does little to sell their attributes. What needs to be remembered at this point is that most people tasked with recruiting new staff have a day job. It is only when they finish their daytime work that they sit down to read the CVs that have been submitted for a role. This is often evening work. Faced with fifty CVs when you are tired can be a daunting task. This is why the applicant needs to present themselves in an attractive and engaging manner. So how is this done in this first opportunity via the CV?

The CV you present needs to be concise and relevant. Normally, it should not exceed a maximum of three pages. The presentation of the information should not appear crammed, nor so detailed that the key points become lost in a fog of words.

We aren't going to discuss how to put together a CV here but there are some key points that need to be highlighted.

A potential employer needs to be able to easily identify the candidate's location, qualifications and a resumé of roles indicating positions, progression and achievements in each. It is often a useful tool as part of a CV to provide an initial paragraph summarising your key achievements and qualities that would identify with the role sought. I have always thought that a final paragraph indicating interests and achievements outside work is useful to a potential employer to obtain a view on the person's overall character.

The CV is simply a tool for potential employers to decide who to call in for interview.
The CV is a useful tool for the candidate to obtain an interview

Letter of application to accompany the CV

Again, this should be seen by the candidate as another useful tool in the box to obtain an interview. In short, it should summarise the key reasons for making the application, the key qualities and experience that would qualify you for the role. The letter should ensure that the recipient is in no doubt of the candidate's enthusiasm for the role and the applicant's capability and commitment to success should they be successful.

Research and preparation

Research into the prospective employer is crucial ahead of the interview. However, this does need highlighting. It is really quite surprising the number of candidates who turn up without having researched the company.

Why would someone apply to join an organisation without thorough research? Without first finding out about the culture, the aspirations, the products and services, the reputation, the goals and ambitions of the organisation, how could a candidate know whether it would be a suitable organisation to join?

On the flip side, how could a candidate know whether they would be a good fit and be able to offer useful expertise to an organisation if they didn't know enough about them?

Employers who are tasked with interviewing candidates look for signals of the candidates' enthusiasm, work ethic, competences, drive and ambition beyond what they say at interview. How well they have prepared is a significant indicator.

The prospective employer

Some indicators a candidate should research about the employer prior to interview:
What do they do?
The Company's mission; their indications, their values; the Company culture; what kind of character? LinkedIn, Facebook; Social events News about the

Company: news feeds, recent success, reviews from clients

Company history: start, growth, new openings, developments, aspirations

Their competitors: who? what are they doing? the industry and developments

The Company USP: what makes them stand out from the other competitors?

Management: any 'stand outs'? who are the key decision makers, what do we know?

I have always recommended that candidates should compile a short presentation, perhaps three or four pages summarising their research which should be bound in a suitable folder. You should carry two or three copies of it to the interview in case there is a panel. This document will continue to sell you long after you have left. It can also put you head and shoulders above other candidates who might not have prepared in the same way.

It is totally within your own interests to research the above information so that you can make an informed decision as to whether the company is right for you.

Having put time into preparation makes for a more meaningful discussion at interview and demonstrates to the decision makers that you are a capable and enthusiastic candidate.

The Interview

Appearance and first impressions

Normally, a decision maker will take a view in the first twenty seconds whether you appear to be the kind of person who would fit in the organisation. This is similar to first impressions at a sales call.

Your appearance should show respect for the post applied for and towards those present. It has been said that you should dress for the role *you aspire to* rather than the one you are in! There is some truth to this. Always ensure that you present yourself in a professional manner. There have been times in the past when I have seen the makings of an excellent candidate yet something in their appearance has let them down. I have on occasion sent candidates to M&S to buy socks when they have presented to me in white ones!

Candidates should carry an appropriate briefcase for their paperwork which in turn should be highly organised as part of the preparation for the interview. When invited to sit during the interview you will be able to take out your documents such as your CV, letter of application and presentation to refer to as required.

Body language and responses

Body language is a very important aspect of the interview and should not be overlooked.
Interviewers will observe the candidate and, in turn, they are conveying their own body language which the candidate can pick up on.

From the moment a candidate arrives at the company they should be aware that the interview has started. Often the decision maker will canvass the opinion of other staff members: the receptionist, the other team members and so on. It is a valuable tip to engage with everyone you meet.
There was an incidence I can recall where a candidate arrived for interview at a company and announced his arrival in reception to the person behind the desk. He was dismissive and somewhat rude in his manner towards this person. He was directed to take a seat and await the interview, only to find that, when called into the office he was greeted by the interviewer - the same person he had been rude to in reception.

When called to the interview provide a strong and engaging handshake and smile.
As you enter the office wait to be asked to be seated and thank your host. Do not invade their space by putting your briefcase or paperwork on their desk. Work from your lap or from your briefcase beside your chair.

As the conversation develops show enthusiasm for points raised, lean forward to make points and engage your interviewer. Be a good listener and think carefully about responses. When there is a pause in the conversation don't be tempted to jump into it! It is important to appear to be considered in your responses.

Handling the interviewer

Surprisingly, it is important for the candidate to gain a measure of control over the interview. It is not all one direction for traffic. It is equally important for the candidate to ascertain whether the company is a good fit for them as much as the other way around.
I have advised applicants in the past to prepare the following to assist them in the conclusion of their interview.

To prepare several key questions about the company and about the role that they would need clarification on.
Prepare SIX reasons why they would be the best candidate for the role. (This could also form part of the presentation we discussed earlier)

Concluding the interview

There is no point in a candidate attempting to come to a decision during the interview whether they believe that the job is good for them and whether they want to pursue it. The interview is the place to secure the role first and foremost. Thinking about it is the luxury afforded to the successful candidate later!
My advice is to go all out to get the job; convince the decision maker that you are the best person for the role and to achieve it.

The conclusion of the interview needs to be controlled in part by the candidate. If the position is a sales role then all the more reason to 'Close for the order'!

The questions you should ask at the conclusion of the interview are:

'So what are your thoughts about my application for the role?'
'What reservations might you have about giving me the job?'   This is your chance to overcome their reservations
'Have I got the job?'

This sounds a little brash but it works!
Even if the decision makers need time to discuss your application you will have done enough to convince them of:

Your enthusiasm for the role
Your tenacity to get it
If the role is a sales role - your ability to close the deal!

Finally, if you really want the job, immediately contact the decision maker by email the same day and confirm your enthusiasm for the role. This will not be lost on the interviewer.

Checklist for a sales interview

Preparation for interview
Presentation with several bound copies
Appearance and professionalism
Body language preparation
Handling the interview and the interviewer
Key questions
The 6 reasons you are the best person for the role
Closing the interview for success - *get the job!*
Confirmation after the interview

Concluding thoughts

I hope this book has provided all that you need to achieve sales success and the motivation for you to go out and find your customers. Keep it with you and dip into it regularly.

There is nothing like the exhilaration of sales success and at the same time there is nothing to surpass providing the solution your client really needs.

My final gift to you is to tell you that, having been engaged in sales throughout my career and having benefited from the best of training, having experienced success in every role I have undertaken, *this* is the key to your success.

Sales is all about building quality relationships. It is about listening carefully to your clients and it is about going the extra mile to provide solutions that meet their requirements. Return regularly to the basic principles of selling as a matter of course. It is these that will be your guide, your mentor and your ultimate success.

The key attributes you need to be successful in sales never change:

The motivation to achieve your goals
Self belief and personal confidence
The desire and willingness to build trustworthy and lasting relationships

To strive to be the best in everything you aspire to do.

About the author

Stephen Carroll is a professional and highly experienced business entrepreneur who has been successful in establishing and growing several high-performing companies, both at home and abroad, demonstrating ability and a 'can-do' attitude. The structured sales, management and business training in his early career created a platform for his own business success and these days he enjoys nothing more than to share some of the experience gained along the way, especially his proven methods to create and develop quality client relationships that lead to new sales and sustainable business. He now consults with small businesses to help them grow in a well organised structure, systems and with trained commercial staff equipped with the right sales and marketing skills for long term business success.

www.ingramcontent.com/pod-product-compliance
Lightning Source LLC
Chambersburg PA
CBHW052357220526
45465CB00003BB/1146